THE
NEW
YOU

GOLDEN LION PUBLICATIONS

Golden Lion Publications © Copyright 2021 - All rights reserved. The content contained within this book may not be reproduced, duplicated or transmitted without direct written permission from the author or the publisher.

Under no circumstances will any blame or legal responsibility be held against the publisher, or author, for any damages, reparation, or monetary loss due to the information contained within this book, either directly or indirectly.

Legal Notice:
This book is copyright protected. It is only for personal use. You cannot amend, distribute, sell, use, quote or paraphrase any part, or the content within this book, without the consent of the author or publisher.

Disclaimer Notice:
Please note the information contained within this document is for educational and entertainment purposes only. All effort has been executed to present accurate, up to date, reliable, complete information. No warranties of any kind are declared or implied. Readers acknowledge that the author is not engaged in the rendering of legal, financial, medical or professional advice. The content within this book has been derived from various sources. Please consult a licensed professional before attempting any techniques outlined in this book.

By reading this document, the reader agrees that under no circumstances is the author responsible for any losses, direct or indirect, that are incurred as a result of the use of the information contained within this document, including, but not limited to, errors, omissions, or inaccuracies.

ISBN: 9798451766552

Contents

Introduction — 13

Diet For Strength Training — 19

Stretching Exercises — 39

Introductory Level Exercises — 64

Beginner Level Exercises — 86

Advanced Level Exercises — 106

Conclusion — 124

References — 126

STRECTHING PROGRAM

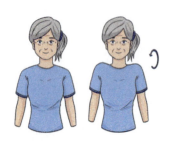

Shoulder Circles

Page:50

Cross-Body Shoulder Stretch

Page:52

Calf Stretch

Page:54

Child's Pose

Page:56

Glute Stretch

Page:58

Downward Dog

Page:60

INTRODUCTORY LEVEL PROGRAM

Push-Ups

Page:72

Lunges

Page:74

Bicycle Curl

Page:76

Chest Fly with Dumbbells

Page:80

Squat with Dumbbells

Page:82

Dumbbell Deadlift

Page:84

BEGINNER LEVEL PROGRAM

The Swan
Page: 92

The Corkscrew
Page: 94

The Roll Over
Page: 96

Shoulder Press
Page: 100

Leg Extension
Page: 102

Barbell Squat
Page: 104

ADVANCED LEVEL PROGRAM

The Rising Swan

Page:110

The Mountain Climber

Page:112

The Boomerang

Page:114

Barbell Bench Press

Page:118

Barbell Heel Raise

Page:120

Barbell Front Squat

Page:122

Introduction

Why would you want to be strong if you're a senior? That is an interesting question, and the answer is largely subjective. Only you can answer as to what a stronger physique means for yourself. Strength means different things to different people, especially after you hit a certain age in your life. The reasons to start strength training later in life can vary from the simple desire to have a better-looking body to improving physical flexibility, reducing the risk of disease and injury, and bringing a sense of order and discipline to day-to-day life. All these reasons are important and valid.

Being healthy and happy is at the heart of strength training, giving you peace of mind and better self-esteem along the way. It adds muscle, reduces fat, and elevates your metabolic rate that usually goes down with age. It also reduces stress and anxieties. There is something about physical exercises and exertion that acts as a release outlet to the pressure of daily life. The discipline that comes with maintaining a regular strength training program tends to seep into other areas of life and improve productivity, and the quality of life in general. Moreover, getting into strength training can be an amazing confidence builder, helping you step outside of your comfort zone and seize the day as it is meant to be.

Improving your overall health is a major benefit of strength training, even when you are lifting weights using your body weight for your exercises. Each year after the ages of 35, you tend to lose a certain amount of bone mass and can be susceptible to brittle bones that bring many potential risks such as fractures and getting a hunched over posture as you age. Strength training can drastically slow the rate of bone loss that comes with age. When you lose excess weight with aerobic exercises such as walking or cycling, you tend to lose your muscle along with the fat that can lead to a drop in your metabolism as well. Strength training focuses on building muscles, which helps maintain and even boost your metabolism, helping you stay toned and healthy at the same time. The weight loss component that comes with strength training helps keep your LDL cholesterol levels low, hence reducing your risk of cardiovascular diseases which are common among the over forty age group.

There are many pursuits in life that you can do haphazardly and still expect good results. Strength training is not one of them. It requires discipline, and a commitment to see things through to the end. When you work with weights, either you lift that dumbbell, or you do not. There is no halfway. What is important, however, is that you start small and work your way towards your best potential. Strength training is a marathon, not a sprint. Once you are in it, you are in it for the long haul. The good thing is when you experience the exhilaration that comes with proper strength training, you will likely not look back.

Let us guide you through the journey of strength training in your senior years, step by step. In the pages ahead, you will see detailed instructions for your strength training, starting from stretching, introductory exercises, beginners exercises, and finally advanced exercises with higher training intensities that will help push your limits and help you discover realms in your mind and the body that you had not explored before. You will also see plenty of safety tips and suggestions to make this journey safe and fun for you.

The human body has several major muscle groups that are targeted during strength training. Being familiar with these muscle groups will help you properly follow the exercise mentioned in this book, and later formulate your own training program.

- *Chest (Pectoral muscles)*

- *Back (Latissimus Dori/trapezius muscles)*

- *Shoulders (Deltoid muscles)*

- *Arms (Biceps/Triceps)*

- *Legs and Calves (Quadriceps, hamstrings, gastrocnemius)*

- *Core (Abdominal muscles)*

There are also smaller and muscle groups that further help you break down your strength training process, especially if you are planning to tone your body to become more aesthetically pleasing. These smaller muscle groups include your glutes (muscles in your hips and butt area), delts (muscles that form the rounded corner of your shoulder), and obliques (muscles located on each side of your abdominal muscles). Your workout cycles should be planned in a way that each of these muscle groups are targeted, in order for you to get the best out of your strength training.

Here are few basic strength training terms that you will see continuously in the book and their meanings:

- *Rep: A repetition or completion of a certain exercise. (One squat, one lunge, one arm curl)*

- *Set: A number of repetitions before you rest. (8-12 reps of squats = 1 set)*

- *Rest interval: The time in between sets to rest your body.*

- *Intensity: The resistance or how hard your body is working during the workout.*

- *Program: The structure of your strength training. This includes a strategic sequence of exercises that will help you reach your desired goal.*

- *Cycle: How strength training programs are segmented.*

Without further ado, let's start!

Introduction | 17

Diet For Strength Training

As we age, the metabolic process in our body naturally slows down. Metabolism is a complex process of biochemical reactions that turn the food we eat into energy, so we can stay active and healthy. Slow metabolic processes mean that our body is unable to efficiently metabolize nutrients from the food we eat. As a result, we tend to lose our muscle mass and it is relatively harder to gain muscle as we get older. Therefore, when you are strength training, it is important to consume food and drinks that help with your metabolism and overall health, while avoiding food that can accelerate the aging process of the body.

What to Eat and Drink to Help With Strength Training

By the time you reach a certain age, you are hopefully aware of the way your body responds to food. You know your likes and dislikes, your body's natural hunger cues and you have a general idea about how your body metabolizes what you eat. Changing your diet when you start strength training during your senior years is less about piling your plate with a bunch of high protein food, and more about adding a variety of food that helps you build lean muscle, with a good understanding of their nutrient profile. Apart from lean proteins, you need a healthy mix of **calcium, iron, vitamin c, vitamin B12, vitamin d, and more** on your plate to give you the energy to persist with strength training, build muscle, and burn unnecessary fat along the way.

What Not to Eat or Drink to Help With Strength Training

Avoiding food that can sabotage your fitness journey is just as important as consuming food that can help you. Any kind of workout routine, especially strength training, requires discipline and self-control. Especially if you have been practicing bad eating habits for the better part of your senior years, it can be difficult to gather the willpower to remove your favorite unhealthy food items from your meals. However, prevention is always better than cure, especially at this age. If the kind of food you are eating is making you sick and sabotaging your strength training, it is time to let them go. With that being said, it is important to know that nobody, not even the dieticians who give you advice, eat perfectly all the time. It is fine to indulge in them as a treat once in a while, however ease off the following food and drinks off your day-to-day meals to stay strong and in good health as you age.

DO EAT

Lean Meats

Lean meat is a source of animal protein with a lower fat and calorie content. Some meats are leaner than others in general, while almost all the popular meats including pork, beef, and lamb have lean cuts that you can opt for over cuts with higher fat content. When it comes to poultry such as chicken and turkey, the skin accounts for most of the fat content. You can add them to your diet by cooking them without the skin and by trimming off any visible fat before you cook. Rabbit and venison are two other lean types of meat that also have high amounts of iron. If you prefer to stick with familiar meats like chicken or steak, opt for chicken breasts and lean cuts like Sirloin tip side steak or top round steak.

DON'T EAT

Deep-Fried Food

Deep frying or submerging a food in hot oil is a common cooking method that gives food a crispy texture, pleasant aroma, and flavor. Some of the popular fried foods include french fries, fried chicken, and cheese sticks. However, deep-frying is one of the unhealthiest ways to eat food since they are high in both calories and trans fat. Excess calories can lead to weight gain, while trans fats can significantly increase your LDL levels. Apart from causing obesity and increasing your risk of heart disease, fried food may contain toxic substances such as acrylamide that can lead to life-threatening diseases such as cancer.

If you must deep fry, use healthy oils with high levels of mono-saturated fats and are stable for high-temperature cooking such as olive oil. Using an air fryer is a good way to achieve the same texture and taste of deep frying without the added fat. You can also oven-fry your food, which includes using very high temperatures (450°F or 232°C) in the oven with a small drizzle of oil to get a deep-fried effect with less oil.

DO EAT

Fish

Fish is one of the best sources of high-quality proteins and healthy fats, which are exactly the kind of nutrients your body needs when you pass the forty-year mark. Apart from being quite flavorful and delicious without having to add too many ingredients, fish is packed with micronutrients that nourish, soothe and heal your body from within. Some of the important micronutrients in fish that would aid proteins in gaining muscle mass include Vitamin D and B2, calcium, phosphorus, iron, zinc, iodine, magnesium, potassium, and most importantly, omega-3 fatty acids that increase your protein synthesis that fuels your muscle growth. Some of the healthiest fish to eat include Cod, Herring, Mahi-mahi, Mackerel, and Rainbow trout. Wild-caught fish often have more minerals, so a trip to your local fishing spot during the weekends will do some wonders for both your mind and the body.

DON'T EAT

Sweetened Food

Many adults do not think much of limiting their sugar consumption, thinking that if they do not eat sugary snacks and candy that are meant for children, they are good. However, there are many sugar-rich foods and snacks that many adults eat which sneak high amounts of sugar into your bloodstream. Some of these tempting sugar foods include sweetened tea, flavored yogurt, sweet protein bars, cupcakes, cookies, and frozen yogurt.

There are many satisfying alternatives to these unhealthy foods. If you have time, brew your own flavored versions of tea without the added sugar that comes with the store-bought options. You would be surprised to find how easy it is to make blueberry, mandarin, or vanilla flavored tea with zero added sugars. Whenever there is a choice, go for the unsweetened and/or the zero-calorie option of the food. If you like your yogurt with a little added flavor, you can top plain Greek yogurt with fresh or dried fruit.

DO EAT

Eggs

Being a senior means that you have already settled into a comfortable rhythm of life. Therefore, as you make your transition towards a healthier life and a stronger body, it is always better to amplify the healthy food choices that you had in your everyday meals already such as eggs. They are inexpensive, widely available, easy to make, and are packed with high-quality proteins and nutrients. Chicken eggs are the closest it gets to a "complete" source of protein. They have all nine essential amino acids that our bodies cannot synthesize from scratch fast enough to supply their demand, therefore we must obtain from our diet. It is, however, important to use a low-calorie cooking method such as boiling or poaching the eggs so you do not add any extra fat calories to the diet.

DON'T EAT

Fizzy Drinks

An occasional fizzy drink with popcorn while you watch Superbowl is harmless enough, however, if you are in the habit of drinking soft drinks daily with your meals, now is a good time to put an end to it. It is the excessive added sugar in soft drinks that can cause harm, especially in the long term. To give some context, an average bottle of fizzy drinks can contain up to 16 teaspoons of sugar. The high fructose syrups in fizzy drinks can only be metabolized by your liver. When you consume them too much, your liver may become overloaded and turn the fructose into fat, which leads to fatty liver disease. Some of the healthier alternatives to fizzy drinks include coconut water, sparkling water, and freshly squeezed lemonade.

DO EAT

Beans and Legumes

With a nice crunchy texture and a pleasant natural flavor to them, beans and other legumes are tiny pods of nutrition that you need to have in your diet. There are a wide variety of legumes you can choose from according to your taste and nutrition preferences, but legumes have been a staple food in many cultures for a reason. They are delicious and are packed with nutrients. Some of the legumes you can add to your diet are beans, peas, lentils, soybeans, and peanuts. They can come in the form of a simple snack to a nice warm bowl of chili that will easily make a meal. Legumes are a great plant-based protein source and have plenty of micronutrients such as iron, folate, magnesium, and potassium. With the high fiber count in legumes, they will help ease the digestion of the high protein meals that you are consuming when you are strength training.

DON'T EAT

Heavily Processed Food

Simply put, "processed food" includes food that has been pre-cooked, frozen, packaged, frozen, preserved, or changed the nutritional composition in some way. Even the wholewheat bread and chopped apples you buy at the grocery store belong to this category, which means that not all processed foods are bad. Processed foods become bad when they are heavily processed in a way that they have gone through complex chemical processes to change the integrity of the food. Heavily processed food, while easy and convenient to consume if you live a busy life, has many potential adverse health effects. Avoid heavily processed food such as frozen food and pre-made meals as much as possible especially during your strength training.

DO EAT

Tofu

If you are willing to add one new food item to your diet as a part of your strength training, it should be tofu. It is a staple in Thai and Chinese cuisine. This high protein food is derived from soybeans, and popularly has no taste, soaking up the flavors of any topping that you add to it. Some of the nutritional highlights of tofu include containing all nine essential amino acids, just like eggs, making it a great protein option for vegans and vegetarians. Apart from helping out with building muscle and giving you energy for strength training, tofu is also believed to help lower bad cholesterol, and even potentially reduce breast cancer by being a natural binder to estrogen receptor sites in human cells due to the phytoestrogens in tofu that have a similar structure to estrogen.

What to Eat to Help With Health in Your Senior Years

One of the signs of aging you may experience is the slower and somewhat weaker response of your immune system. Your risk of getting sick is higher than when you were younger, and it may take a little longer for you to heal from even a common cold. There is also a larger risk to develop autoimmune diseases, conditions in which your immune system mistakenly attacks your body. Oxidative stress or the imbalance between free radicals and antioxidants in your body is another major cause of diseases such as diabetes, cancer, rheumatoid arthritis, cardiovascular diseases, and more. Therefore, it is extremely important to include immune-boosting and antioxidant-rich food in your day-to-day meals.

Whole Grains

A grain is made of three parts, the bran, the germ, and the endosperm. Whole-grain foods are made of grains that have all three of those parts intact. Refined grains such as white flour have a smoother texture and flavor, but they are devoid of a score of nutrients packed in the bran and the germ. Whole grains have fiber, B vitamins, antioxidants, and a lot of trace minerals such as iron, zinc, and magnesium. While the taste of whole grain food can be coarse to some degree, making the switch from refined grains to whole grains can have a huge impact on your health, especially during your senior years. Some of the most common whole grains you can easily incorporate into your diet, especially your breakfast and side dishes, include oatmeal, quinoa, brown rice, barley, and buckwheat. Also, make sure you go for whole grain options whenever you buy bread and cereal.

Nuts and Seeds

If there is one illness that is largely common among seniors, it is high cholesterol levels, which is a major risk factor for heart disease. The reason for this commonality is mostly unhealthy dietary habits and inactive lifestyles. Cholesterol is a type of lipid which is vital for certain cellular functions in our body. They come in two major forms, LDL and HDL. When it comes to dietary fat, there are also two different forms—"good" or unsaturated fats, and "bad" or trans/saturated fats. Nuts and Seeds, for the most part, contain healthy fats. They are also free of dietary cholesterol, and high in dietary fiber that can reduce the absorption of cholesterol into your bloodstream. As a bonus, nuts and seeds are crunchy and delicious unlike many healthier food choices out there, and you can add them as a topping to many dishes to make them healthier and add an extra level of crunchy texture.

Leafy Greens

"Let thy greens be thy medicine, and thy medicine be thy greens". Leafy greens are quite literally one of the most nutrient-dense food groups on the planet. They are filled with amino acids, fiber, iron, magnesium, potassium, folic acid, phytonutrients such as beta-carotene and carotenoids, and a whole lot of vitamins. If there is one item of food you are going to add to your diet from this list, let it be leafy green vegetables. Kale is perhaps the most popular leafy green that was recently popularized by celebrities on social media. Kale is rich in antioxidants, minerals, and vitamins, and best consumed raw. If you are not into eating raw greens, Collard greens are a classic option, a thick loose-leaf green vegetable that can be cooked using moist heat until they are tender. There are also microgreens, young leafy greens that are often used as a garnish or for decoration, a great way to improve the leafy green content in your meals. You can grow microgreens in your backyard all year long as well.

Green Tea

Originated in China, the history of green tea goes back thousands of years. It is one of the healthiest beverages you can consume and slightly nutty bittersweet taste that is pleasant both hot and cold. You can brew a pot of green tea in the morning and taste a warm cup to wake you up, and put the rest in a bottle and drink throughout the day to keep yourself hydrated and help prevent fatigue, stress, and also helsp improve your metabolism. It is loaded with antioxidants that may improve your brain function and lower your risk of heart disease. Green tea has many powerful bioactive compounds that help treat a variety of diseases. The caffeine in green works as a mild stimulant without adverse effects of coffee such as restlessness and increased heart rate.

Fresh Fruit

You know the fun old saying, "an apple a day keeps the doctor away". A list of healthy food choices is definitely incomplete without fresh fruit in it. They can instantly elevate your healthy diet and make it more colorful, flavorful, and joyful. Eating whole fruits helps you stay hydrated, control your blood pressure, and even help retain your muscle mass due to the high level of vitamin C they carry. Fresh fruits are also a great source of natural antioxidants, and they have healthy soluble fiber that improves your digestion and lowers the risk of heart disease. An important thing to remember, however, is to limit the consumption of sugary and overly ripened fruits since your body can hold on to the glucose and fructose sugars in the fruit and increase the risk of diabetes. Keep it to one glass of fruit smoothies or one or two cups of fresh fruit per day.

Stretching Exercises

"You are only as young as your spine is flexible." - Joseph Pilates

Think about that slow stretch of the body you do right after you get up in the morning. How good does that feel? Stretching is a great way to warm up the muscles, get rid of stiffness, improve circulation, and release endorphins that reduce pain and boost pleasure. We do it naturally and even involuntarily since we were babies. In fact, humans are not the only animals who love a good stretch. If you have a cat or a dog, you have probably seen them stretching after a good nap, or even when they are feeling bored after sitting somewhere for too long. Stretching is nature's reset button. It awakens your body and relaxes tight and stiff muscles. Especially as you age, it is important to include stretching in your day-to-day life, since it will reduce pains and help you stay flexible and active.

What Happens When You Stretch?

Stretching involves deliberately straightening or extending your body parts to their full length, or as much as you are able to extend them. You have over 600 muscles in your body. They are made of fibrous, elastic tissue. Muscle tissue contains muscle fibers, each consisting of a single muscle cell. These fibers can contract, relax, and elongate. When you stretch, your muscle fiber is pulled to its full length. This helps your muscle to realign any disorganized fibers in the direction of any tension or stiffness you have. This realignment is what helps nurse any scarred tissue back to health when you recover from a muscle injury. It also helps heal and recover the muscles that get fatigued often as you age.

When you stretch your muscles, depending on their location in your body, some of their fibers lengthen and some of them remain at rest. The length of your muscle depends upon the number of stretched fibers at any given time. As you learn about the importance of stretching, it is also important to understand the way our brain and the neural components adapt to stretching. When your muscles stretch, the nerve control points that are located among the groups of muscles called muscle spindles also stretch. The function of these muscle spindles is to protect the body from injury and maintain the tone of the muscle. They record the way the length of the muscle changes due to stretching and signals the brain, triggering the stretch reflex which contracts the muscle. When you stretch suddenly, these muscle contractions will be strong and uncomfortable. This is why you have to ease into your stretching.

Benefits of Stretching as A Senior

It is natural to lose some of the functionality you enjoyed in your bright-eyed and bushy-tailed younger years once you become a senior. As a part of the aging process, your muscles become less elastic, and you cannot lengthen them as you used to. However, the ability of your muscles to be trained does not stop with age. If you put some time every day into helping them be more flexible, especially with resistance training preceded and followed by a full-body stretching session, you can prolong the time your muscles stay young and healthy. In fact, stretching and strength training are proven to minimize your age-related muscle loss and bone-related disorders.

Reduces Your Risk of Injury

When your body is warmed up and flexible, it is less likely that you would get injured when you work out or do any type of excessive movement. Stretching helps increase your range of movement, and it also helps decrease any resistance your muscles have, making it easier for you to do more intense strength training exercises. When you stretch both sides of your body, you are also helping remedy any muscular imbalances you have, further reducing muscle cramps and similar painful contractions.

Makes Your Body More Flexible and Pliable

Aging often makes your joints and muscles stiff which leads to less flexibility. Stretching is an effective way to improve it, since it increases the length your muscle can lengthen, helping you move with ease. When you stretch, your muscles' temporality lengthens, and it comes back to their normal length automatically. When you do not move your muscles much, they become more and more resistant to being stretched. Practicing stretching regularly keeps your muscles ready and improves their elasticity which you can then use for more intense exercises such as strength training.

Helps Reduce Stress

Relieving muscle tension directly impacts your mental state. Stretching, when done properly, is similar to a massage to your sore joints and muscles. A good stretching session often takes time, and it allows you to connect with your body and for your thoughts to slow down. As you relieve the stress that you are carrying on your muscles when you stretch, you are also entering a meditative state that relieves your mental stress as well. Reducing stress from both your body and mind helps you sleep better as well.

Reduces Age-Related Aches and Pains

Stretching increases the blood flow to your muscles and improves your circulation overall. This helps the muscles to receive more oxygen and get rid of any metabolic waste products that are causing discomfort. It also releases endorphins, a chemical that is produced in your central nervous system that have great pain-relieving effects.

Improves Your Posture

You are putting your muscles to work when you stretch. You are lengthening them, strengthening them, and basically making them do their job that they do not get to do due to the inactive modern lifestyles that we live. As a result, you will use any tightness or awkward muscle tensions that lead to bad posture. Stretching pulls your spine into positions that help it make better connections with your back, neck, and core muscles, giving you a better posture. With regular stretching, you will notice that you are able to sit up straight with comfort and stand tall with good posture and a straight back.

Safety Tips

If you are new to working out and conscious stretching that warms you up for the more intense exercises that come after, there are quite a few safety tips that you should know beforehand. If you stretch incorrectly, the chances are that it will do more harm than good.

Here are some tips for safe stretches:

You Need To Warm Up Before Stretching

Since stretching is considered a warm-up, many people tend to plunge right into stretching before a workout. However, stretching cold muscles can lead to painful strains. Before you start your stretching session, do some light walking, jogging, or using an elliptical bike at low intensity for about ten minutes to warm up your muscles. Just like taffy, warm muscles are easier to stretch!

Aiming For Pain Is Bad

One of the most harmful beliefs in the fitness community is that if you feel pain, then you are doing a good job. This is not true when it comes to stretching. Your aim should be to feel mild to moderate tension when you stretch. The moment you start feeling pain, hold the stretch. You can try to reset your position carefully and then try again if you wish, but do not try to push through the pain. Do not worry. With constant and consistent practice along with strength training, your flexibility will inevitably improve.

Symmetry Is Key

Our bodies naturally change as we age, and losing flexibility is often a part of it. When you are getting into strength training after the age of 40, it is always important to keep your expectations attainable. This applies to stretching as well. If you strive to be as flexible as a twenty-year-old ballet dancer when you stretch, it is likely that you will get hurt and discouraged soon. Your focus should be to attain equal flexibility on both sides of your body. When your flexibility is not equal, it can be a risk factor when you are strength training later on.

Avoid Bouncing

A common mistake that beginners tend to make when stretching is making bounce motions to extend the stretch. This can be harmful and lead to injuries. It's okay to make gentle movements which help improve your balance, but avoid rigid and bouncy movements when you stretch. Take your time with the stretch and be smooth when you move while keeping a steady posture. Do not try to rush through your stretching session before the workout. In fact, the longer you take, the less pain and resistance you will feel when you do your strength training.

Remember To Breathe

Breathe. Inhale and exhale consciously and with purpose when you stretch. Deep breathing lowers stress and stabilizes your blood pressure, which is extremely important before you move onto more intense strength training workouts.

STRECTHING PROGRAM

Shoulder Circles

Cross-Body Shoulder Stretch

Calf Stretch

Child's Pose

Glute Stretch

Downward Dog

Lateral Raise & External

Rotation

Shoulder Circles

BEGINNER

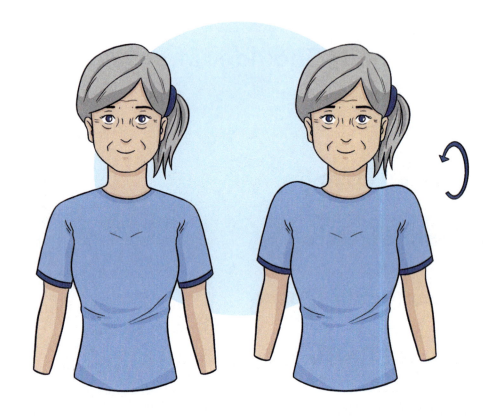

NO-EQUIPMENT

Instructions

1. Stand or sit in a neutral position with your back straight. Pull your shoulders back and open up your chest. Inhale deeply and exhale fully. Let your body feel heavy and relaxed.

2. Raise your shoulders and rotate them slowly forward. Do up to 10 reps, or until you feel a stretch in your triceps. Pause, relax for a moment.

3. Repeat the exercise in reverse.

This is an easy upper body stretch to get you warmed up. It helps relax and build muscle tone in your shoulder area, triceps and biceps. You can do it either standing or sitting, and it is discreet enough to do even at your work.

Upper Body Stretching | 51

Cross-Body Shoulder Stretch

BEGINNER

NO-EQUIPMENT

Instructions

1. Stand tall or sit with your back straight. Relax your body. Inhale and exhale.

2. Bring one arm in front of you. Use the opposite hand to grab your elbow, and pull it across your body towards your chest.

3. Move the opposite hand from your elbow towards the shoulder, and gently press until you feel the stretch in your shoulder.

4. Keep your elbow slightly below your shoulder height and pause for 10 -30 seconds.

5. Repeat on the other side.

This is another upper-body stretch that warms up your shoulders, arms, and chest. You can do it while sitting or standing, but make sure you keep your back and chin straight for better posture and results.

CALF STRETCH
BEGINNER

NO-EQUIPMENT

Instructions

1. Stand tall with your feet shoulder-width apart. Relax your body.

2. Step your right foot forward, and keep your left foot firmly on the ground.

3. Bend your right foot forward until you feel the stretch on your calf muscles. Do not move your knee past your ankle. Hold for up to 30 seconds, or as long as you can.

4. Switch and repeat.

This is a classic exercise that targets your calf muscles and requires zero equipment. If you think of your body as a house, your lower body is the strong foundation that holds the rest of it. By warming up, you can avoid and reduce the pains and discomforts that may occur during strength training.

Child's Pose

BEGINNER

Apart from all the stretching benefits, Child's pose is great as a stress reliever and an easy remedy for back pain.

NO-EQUIPMENT

Instructions

1. Kneel on a mat with your thighs perpendicular to the floor, your shins parallel to the floor, and your head facing forward.

2. Slowly put your feet together behind you, with your toes touching each other.

3. Lower your hip backward as far as you can, and sit on your heels. Rest your belly on your thighs.

4. Extend your arms in front of you, and slowly rest your forehead on the floor.

5. Fully give into the long stretch from top to bottom, and let your shoulders and the back fully feel the stretch. Deepen the stretch as much as you can. Relax your body.

6. Hold for up to 30 seconds, or for as long as you feel good.

Glute Stretch

BEGINNER

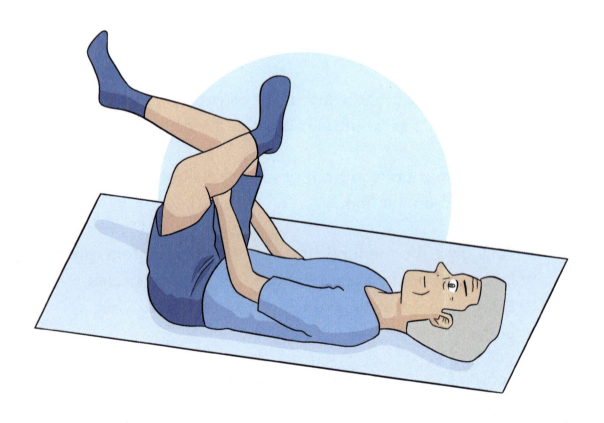

NO-EQUIPMENT

Instructions

1. Lie on your back and relax your body. Fill your lungs with a full inhale and exhale fully.

2. Bring your legs up until your toes point to the ceiling, and bend your knees at 90 degrees.

3. Use your hands to place your left ankle over your right knee.

4. Hold your right leg firmly behind your knee, and pull it towards your face. Feel the stretch on your glutes.

5. Hold for 30 seconds. Switch legs and repeat.

This stretching exercise targets your glutes and hips. You can do this both before and after your strength training to ease any aches and pains, removing any remaining tension on your back.

Downward Dog

BEGINNER

Apart from building strength, this stretch also increases your flexibility and relieves back pain. Make sure you do some initial upper and lower body warm-up exercises before you attempt this full-body stretch.

NO-EQUIPMENT

Instructions

1. Get into a push-up position, with your legs together and your hands kept firmly on the floor shoulder-width apart.

2. Keep your body straight and your core fully engaged. In that position, slowly move your hips up, forming a V shape with your body, like a mountain. You can slightly bend your knees if you feel too much discomfort.

3. Lower your head and place between your shoulders while keeping your body steady. Feel your body stretch from your neck to your toes. Deepen your stretch by raising your heels.

4. Hold the pose for 20-30 seconds. Return to your starting position.

Lateral Raise & External Rotation

BEGINNER

EQUIPMENT

Instructions

1. Stand tall and let your arms drop either side of you. Take a deep breath and exhale slowly.

2. Grab your light dumbbells and hold them at arm's length.

3. Bend your elbows 90 degrees. Turn your palms towards each other firmly holding dumbbells.

4. Slowly raise your upper arms to the sides until they are at your chest height and parallel to the floor.

5. Rotate your upper arms towards up, and then back, so your forearms are pointed towards the ceiling. Pause.

6. Reverse the movement and return to your starting position. Repeat.

Upper Body Stretching | 63

Introductory Level Exercises

This chapter is for complete novices to strength training who have never lifted weights before. Also, if you have lifted weights in your early twenties, but have not touched a dumbbell in well over twenty years, make sure you read this chapter to refresh your mind about the basics of weight training. Throughout the book, you will see plenty of exercise options, covering your upper body, lower body, and full body. Using free weights is arguably the more superior method for building strength. However, the book includes workout options both using equipment and without, which you can combine and customize when you put together your own strength training program.

At the end of each chapter, there is a common workout program that calls for training 3 days per week, which is ideal for getting visible results without delay. You do not need to get into that program right away, especially if you are not working out under the supervision of a trainer. Start slowly, and work your way up to that level. The exact days you will be working out is completely up to you, but always leave at least one rest day in between each training day to allow recovery. Your body needs plenty of rest and sufficient nutrition in order to become stronger as a result of your strength training. Be persistent and consistent until these introductory level exercises feel natural and easy by which point you can move to the next stage.

Basic Training Equipment

Being too overwhelmed by the different types of weight training equipment is one of the biggest reasons people do not get into strength training. However, when you have a clear target and a basic understanding of your capabilities, it is not too difficult to choose your training equipment. In fact, you do not need weights to engage in strength training at all.

Using weights for better resistance is only one type of strength training. You are simply using free weights or other equipment such as resistance bands, tubing, or a weight machine to create stress to the muscles, gradually improving their strength. The same results can be achieved by a no-equipment strength training method such as pilates, which uses your own bodyweight to achieve the same results. If you are new to strength training, however, using free weights or similar equipment can often speed up the results.

Here are some common strength training tools that you can include in your basic kit for introductory exercises.

Introductory Level Exercises | 65

Free weights

These are individual objects that are not fastened to anything such as dumbbells, barbells, bars, and weight plates. You can pick them up and freely move around. They come in a wide range of shapes, sizes, and weights. You can start with a small size and weight, and increase as you progress.

Resistance Bands

These are relatively new in the fitness world. They are bands made of a strong rubber material that can be stretched by putting physical effort. They are affordable, lightweight, and great for strength training beginners and frequent travelers who want a portable tool that will help keep up with their training when they are traveling.

Weight Training Machines

If you prefer doing your strength training in a gym, you can use a weight training machine such as a Leg Press, a Chest Press, or an indoor rowing machine. They usually have a seat, movable bar, and a cable or a pulley with various weight plates to adjust the resistance and intensity. There are new and sophisticated machines that come with digital features that will give you specific feedback when you are training.

Exercise Balls

Large inflatable balls that give a bouncy surface on which you can work out, exercise balls give a sense of instability that increases the difficulty level and intensity of your weight training, which leads to deeper use of your back and abdominal muscles.

"For me life is continuously being hungry. The meaning of life is not simply to exist, to survive, but to move ahead, to go up, to achieve, to conquer."

- Arnold Schwarzenegger

Introductory Level Program

Push-Ups

Lunges

Bicycle Curl

Chest Fly with Dumbbells

Squat with Dumbbells

Dumbbell Deadlift

Push-Ups

INTRODUCTORY

Tips and Notes!

Your body should maintain a straight position throughout the exercise to achieve the optimal tension on your targeted muscles. As you inhale and exhale, concentrate and be aware of how your abdominal muscles contract. Once you have your form right, increase your reps.

NO-EQUIPMENT

Instructions

1. Lower your body on to the yoga mat and assume a high-plant position with your shoulders, hips, knees and feet in a straight line. Keep your hands comfortably shoulder width apart. You should feel the tension of your weight on your palms and toes, but there should be no pain or excessive discomfort.

2. Maintain your steady and straight body position, and lower your chest toward the floor. Inhale during the lowering movement.

3. Raise your body up until your arms are extended fully, and come back to the starting position.

4. Exhale as you come up.

Lunges

INTRODUCTORY

It is important that your knee does not extend further than your foot in order to keep the stress minimal at the knee joint.

NO-EQUIPMENT

Instructions

1. Stand tall with your back straight and your feet hip-width apart. Look straight ahead and push your shoulders back.

2. Step your right foot forward and make it as long as possible while keeping your balance.

3. Bend your knee at a 90 degree angle, as if you are kneeling. Your knee should ideally be directly above your foot. Make sure to inhale as you go.

4. Return to the starting position by pushing off your right foot and raising your body up to the initail standing position. Exhale as you go.

5. Alternate your lead foot for each set.

Bicycle Curl

INTRODUCTORY

Tips and Notes!

The goal of the exercise is for your elbow to touch the opposite knee, but it can take some time to build up your body to achieve that Give your body the time to become flexible.

NO-EQUIPMENT

Instructions

1. Lie down on the floor with your face up. Place your hands behind your head and cradle the back of your head comfortably on your hands to maintain a neutral neck position.

2. Raise your upper back off the floor about 30 degrees. This is the "trunk-curled" position that you will maintain throughout the entire exercise.

3. Lift both legs off the floor, to a comfortable height. Left your left leg in, and keep the right leg straight.

4. Twist your upper body to the left, in order for your right elbow to touch your left knee.

5. Alternate legs and repeat.

Introductory Strength Training Exercise With Equipment

Using free weights and other strength training tools when you work out help easily improve your muscle strength, power, and speed. While using your own body weight and lifting weights both help with your muscular endurance and increase your strength, using external resistance often helps with the consistency of the exercise. Moreover, as you move along in your strength training, having external tools makes it easier to level up your resistance than merely utilizing your body weight. With that being said, both methods are able to target all parts of the body to give a well-rounded strength workout. A well-balanced strength training routine includes exercise both with and without equipment.

Chest Fly with Dumbbells

INTRODUCTORY

EQUIPMENT

Instructions

1. Lie down face up on a horizontal gym bench. Relax your body.

2. Straddle the bench securely with your legs and keep your feet flat on the floor. Flex your knees steadily at 90 degrees.

3. Hold the dumbbells on your hands with palms facing each other and raise your hands above your chest, extending as far as you can manage with the weight.

4. Keep your elbows flexed and lower your dumbbells making a wing/flying motion until your arms are extended on either side of you.

5. Inhale deeply as you lower your dumbbells.

6. Bring arms back to the starting position above you, with dumbbells and palms facing each other. Exhale fully as you go.

Squat with Dumbbells

INTRODUCTORY

EQUIPMENT

Instructions

1. Hold your dumbbells with your palms facing toward your body using an overhand grip.

2. Keep your feet hip-width apart and stand tall with your back straight.

3. With your head up and eyes looking ahead, slowly squat down. Your thighs should ideally be parallel to the floor.

4. Your back should be straight and the weight of the dumbbells should equally go to both your feet. Inhale as you squat down.

5. Begin the upward movement by slowly straightening the knees and hips and exhaling.

Tips and Notes!

One of the most common mistakes people make when doing squats is moving their knees forward too much which can cause injuries. Keep your eyes forward at all times to maintain good posture and balance.

Lower Body Workout | 83

Dumbbell Deadlift

INTRODUCTORY

EQUIPMENT

Instructions

1. Use the overhand grip to hold your dumbbells firmly on each hand, and stand tall with your back straight.

2. Keep your head up and feet about hip-width apart.

3. Flex your knees and hips. Rotate the dumbbells so your palms are facing your legs.

4. Rise slowly to a standing position by extending the knees, hips, and trunk. Exhale throughout the upward movement.

5. Return slowly to the starting position with the dumbbells on the floor. Inhale throughout the downward movement.

Tips and Notes!

Maintaining straight back posture is the most important thing to remember when doing this exercise. Do not round your back, especially at the beginning of the exercise. The knees should be over the feet rather than extended forward.

Beginner Level Exercises

The Beginner Level Exercises introduced in this chapter are a few steps beyond the Introductory Level you just completed. Make sure you are fully familiar and confident with one level before you move forward to the next. At this level, you are familiar with your body and are aware of how flexible you are, how much energy you need, and the intensity at which you can perform your strength training workouts. Beginner level exercises are more complex, and more free-weight movements than the introductory level. Free weights are an integral part of strength training programs, and they help you get into more advanced machine exercises with good form and confidence.

Beginner Level Strength Training Exercises Without Equipment

In order to build muscle, you need to challenge the muscle. As you already know, this can be achieved by using your own body weight as leverage. Most of the strength training exercises without equipment that are mentioned here have been inspired by the Pilates exercises. Pilates exercises use your body weight to lengthen, stretch and increase the range of motion of all the major muscle groups in your body. They improve your strength as well as your flexibility and also give you a better command of your body awareness and balance. They make great strength training exercises without the use of any extra tools, they have minimal impact on your joints which make them great for seniors.

The beginner level strength training exercises without equipment that are mentioned in this chapter increase your muscle strength and tone all over your body, particularly of your abdominal muscles, lower back, hips, and buttocks (the 'core muscles' of your body). They help achieve a balanced muscular strength on both sides of your body and enhance muscular control of your back and limbs. They also improve the stabilization of your spine and improve your posture.

"The clock is ticking.
Are you becoming
the person you want
to be?"

- Greg Plitt, Fitness Model

Beginner Level Program

The Swan

The Corkscrew

The Roll Over

Shoulder Press

Leg Extension

Barbell Squat

The Swan

BEGINNER

With consistent practice, this exercise will help you reduce back pain by making your back and upper spine area muscles strong. Since this exercise improves your hip joint flexibility, this exercise is great before you do more intense workouts such as Barbell Squat.

NO-EQUIPMENT

Instructions

1. Lie down on your stomach on a mat.

2. Raise yourself up by pressing your hands down to the mat, and your elbows pushing back. Your chest and the upper spine should be off the mat and raised in an upward arc, like a swan.

3. Once you are comfortable with the starting position, straighten your arms and raise the rest of your spine and hips away from the mat. Your thighs should be off the mat and be a part of the raised swan pose along with your upper body. Pause and take a deep breath at the top.

4. Exhale and slowly lower your body back to the starting position. If you have made it to the full swan, start lowering your body from your thighs, then hips, abdominal muscles, and finally your chest.

Tips and Notes!

When you are in form, your hips should feel fully stretched and when you arch your upper body away from the floor, extend your spine evenly to avoid any discomfort later.

The Corkscrew

BEGINNER

The rhythmic movement stretches your hip flexors and gives a pleasing massage to your lower body while engaging the muscles.

NO-EQUIPMENT

Instructions

1. Take a deep breath in. Keep your belly scooped in and lift your legs up and to the side of your body. Both legs should stay together.

2. With your legs together, draw a circle with your legs with the center being above your belly. Be careful not to lower your legs too much. Keep your upper body calm and stable as much as possible. You can use the back of your arms to press down on the mat to get momentum.

3. Move your legs downwards on the circle, and take them up completing the circle.

4. When you are comfortable with making a circle with your hips staying on the mat, you can increase the force and slightly move your hip upwards when you draw the upper arc of the circle to get a nice lower back massage.

5. Once you complete the circle on one side, you can change the direction and repeat. Continue to move until you have done two to three arcs on each side.

The Roll Over

BEGINNER

Tips and Notes!

The aim of the exercise is to strengthen your core. If you try to flop or tip over in the process, you can hurt your neck and back.

NO-EQUIPMENT

Instructions

1. Take a deep breath in and extend your legs straight up. Your legs should make a 90-degree angle with the floor. and kept firmly together. Point your toes toward the ceiling to make it easier to maintain the starting position.

2. Tilt your pelvis backward and lift your legs as you slowly exhale.

3. Extend your legs in the side of your head and try to reach them over your head. Press your hands down to help with the pelvis and legs. Pay attention to your core muscles and engage them.

4. Lower your legs to the starting position.

Tips and Notes!

Always remember, use the core muscles when you are raising and lowering your legs, not momentum.

Beginner Level Strength Training Exercise With Equipment

At this stage, you can slowly work your way towards using barbells, the ultimate strength training tool in a gym. A barbell is a metal bar that is able to be loaded with weights. When barbell training, one thing to keep in mind though, is some barbells already come in a pre-made weight and aren't adjustable. Barbells can appear intimidating at first due to their bulky appearance, but once you get familiar with dumbbells, making the transition to barbells is far easier than you would think. It is, however, extremely important that you use the correct form when you do your strength training workouts using barbells. Therefore, make sure you get a professional trainer, or an experienced workout partner to spot you when you are using barbells.

Shoulder Press

BEGINNER

EQUIPMENT

Instructions

1. Adjust the seat so that the handles are below chin level; sit with your head, shoulders, and back pressed against the seat pad; and place your feet flat on the floor.

2. Grasp the handles so that the palms are facing away.

3. Push the handles slowly upward until the arms are fully extended. Keep the wrists straight and exhale throughout the pushing movement.

4. Return the handles slowly to the starting position. Inhale throughout the lowering movement.

Tips and Notes!

Using the horizontal handles is more effective for strengthening the deltoid muscles. But if this variation stresses your shoulder joints, reduce the movement range, use the vertical handles, or do both. To reduce the risk of shoulder injuries, stop the downward movement between the chin and clavicles.

Leg Extension

BEGINNER

You should not feel any tension or pain in your knees.

EQUIPMENT

Instructions

1. Sit comfortably on the padded seat with your knees in line with the axis. Most resistance machines have a red dot that indicates rotation.

2. Your back should be firmly against the pad of the seat, and your ankles behind the roller pad.

3. Flex your knees 90 degrees and grip the handles for support.

4. Take a breath in, and as you exhale, use your ankles to push the roller pad until your knees are fully extended.

5. Lower the roller pad to the starting position. Inhale as you do so.

Tips and Notes!

You should always extend your legs until your knees are fully extended. Then, make sure your back is straight and against the back of the seat and not arched in any way.

Barbell Squat

BEGINNER

Start with the lowest weight until you feel comfortable and you are confident with your form. Take your time.

EQUIPMENT

Instructions

1. Place your feet shoulder-width apart. Place them slightly wider for better steadiness if needed. Grip the bar with your fingers going over it.

2. The position of the bar should be on the shoulders and upper back, just below the base of your neck.

3. Stand tall and look ahead. Straighten your knees and lift the bar off the rack.

4. Steady the barbell on your back. Keep looking ahead and your back straight. Balance the weight on both feet, engaging the entire feet throughout the exercise.

5. Squat down slowly, until your thighs become parallel to the floor. Inhale as you go down.

6. Come back to the starting position by slowly straightening your knees and then hips. Exhale as you go upward. After you complete a set, return the barbell back to the rack.

Advanced Level Exercises

After completing your introductory and beginner level exercises, now you have gotten into a steady strength training routine. You are more knowledgeable about using resistance exercises to improve your endurance, and you have a stronger and more flexible body. At this point, you are prepared to start a true strength program with advanced workouts. If there is one thing to keep reminding yourself of at this level, it is that technique is key. You need proper form and technique to avoid any injuries from happening, and without it, your entire process would be stagnated and unsuccessful.

Practise makes perfect, and more importantly, practice makes your results permanent. You are likely experiencing improvements not only in your physical appearance and energy levels but also in your mind. You are more focused, attentive, confident, and motivated. Your introductory and beginner levels are better done with a qualified trainer to spot you, guide you, and perfect your technique. If you continue with poor technique, it will ultimately cause irreversible damage, and make it difficult to correct your mistakes. Always listen to your body. Learn how to understand the difference between the pain that is asking you to stop what you are doing, and the strain that is showing you that you are making progress. Take your time. You are running a marathon, not a sprint!

Advanced Level Program

The Rising Swan

The Mountain Climber

The Boomerang

Barbell Bench Press

Barbell Heel Raise

Barbell Front Squat

The Rising Swan

ADVANCED

The Rising Swan is a good exercise to improve the posture when sitting and to heal any tightness or pain caused by prolonged sitting. It also strengthens your abdominals, pelvic floor, and glutes. If you are a jogger or a runner, this exercise improves your hip joint flexibility. It will also make it easier for you to do workouts with equipment by improving your flexibility.

NO-EQUIPMENT

Instructions

1. Lie down comfortably on your stomach. Lift your upper body until your belly button is lifted away from the mat. This position should be maintained throughout the website, with your abdominal muscles lifted away.

2. Take a deep breath in. Press your forearms down on the mat and lengthen your spine resembling the upper body of a swan. Create a long upward arc from your body. Your head should be in line with your spine, and the elbows should be firm and closer to the body. Push your tailbone toward the map and make sure the hip stays on the map.

3. Release your upper body arc as you exhale, but keep your abdominal muscles lifted. Return your torso to the mat slowly and sequentially.

4. Maintain a deep, even, and flowing breath that supports the movement throughout.

5. Once you complete a set, finish by bending your knees and the rounded and rested on your thighs.

The Mountain Climber

ADVANCED

Tips and Notes!

A common mistake that can happen is bouncing on your toes when performing the climbing move. While it may feel like you are working harder as you bounce, it leads to not getting proper core engagement for the move.

NO-EQUIPMENT

Instructions

1. Get into a plank position, making sure to distribute your weight evenly between your hands and your toes. Your hands should be about shoulder-width apart, back flat, abs engaged, and head in alignment.

2. Pull your right knee into your chest as far as you can.

3. Switch legs, pulling one knee out and bringing the other knee in.

4. Keep your hips down, run your knees in and out as far and as fast as you can. Alternate inhaling and exhaling with each leg change.

The Boomerang

ADVANCED

This is an advanced strength training exercise that combines several Pilates moves that are used in classic mat sequences. It uses several skills that creates a flawless sequence of moves that targets muscle groups all over the body.

NO-EQUIPMENT

Instructions

1. Sit tall on your sit bones with your legs outstretched and crossed.

2. Seal your legs together and feel the sense of midline moving from your legs up your spine and through the top of your head. Maintaining that feeling as you move will help you keep the boomerang shape and give you a line of energy to move along.

3. Place your hands on the mat by your sides.

4. Take your body into a Pilates C-curve.

5. Exhale: Deepen your C-curve and roll back, taking your crossed legs overhead as you would in the rollover exercise. Your body has taken a boomerang shape and will keep that shape through the exercise.

6. You are between your shoulders; the backs of your arms press against the mat, adding stability.

7. At the top of the roll, uncross your legs and re-cross with the other leg on top.

Full Body Workout| 115

    It is easier to remember this workout like choreography and you can put on your favorite music to make the experience even more fun and enjoyable. The "Roll Over" exercise you did in the earlier level is also a part of this exercise. Once you complete this full workout from the beginning to the end, it's quite possible that you would work up a good sweat in the end. When done properly and practised consistently, this exercise will build flexibility and strength throughout your core area and the back, giving you good posture. It is also great for toning and strengthening your legs and improving your overall balance and coordination of the body.

8. Inhale: Bring your whole body up to the teaser position. Keep your boomerang shape. This is an abdominal control move—not a drop of the legs and then a regroup.

9. Continue the inhale as you hold your teaser shape and sweep your arms around to the back. Keep your arms high and perform it with your palms up.

10. Exhale: Stay in control of the shape as you smoothly let your legs come down and sweep your arms wide to the sides.

11. Continue your exhale as you let your arms come all the way to the front (shoulders down, neck long) as you curve over your legs and prepare to begin the sequence again.

12. Start from here with a deep scoop of the belly. Your hands can come back to the mat along your sides to help you.

Barbell Bench Press

ADVANCED

A classic high power upper body strength training exercise, the bench press highly effective and versatile in its benefits. It increases your upper body push strength, which is an important factor and skill for all strength training exercises. It tones and builds up your pecs, which will make your body look youthful and attractive.

EQUIPMENT

Instructions

1. Lie supine with the legs straddling the bench, the knees flexed at 90 degrees, and the feet flat on the floor.

2. Grasp the barbell in an overhand grip with the palms facing away and press the bar until the arms are fully extended above the chest.

3. Lower the bar slowly and evenly to the chest.

4. Inhale throughout the lowering movement.

5. Press the bar upward evenly until the arms are fully extended. Exhale throughout the pressing movement.

Tips and Notes!

Before you attempt this exercise, make sure your bench has secure uprights to hold the bar. You also need a trained spotter to get you through the exercise safely and effectively.

Barbell Heel Raise

ADVANCED

EQUIPMENT

Instructions

1. Remove the barbell from the rack and assume a position with the bar on your shoulders, then move the bar to the base of your neck.

2. Place the balls of the feet on a stable elevated surface approximately 2 inches high, about hip-width apart and parallel to each other.

3. Keep the head up, eyes fixed straight ahead, shoulders back, back straight, and weight on the balls of the feet throughout the upward and downward movement phases of this exercise.

4. Rise up slowly onto the toes while keeping the torso erect and the knees straight. Exhale throughout the upward movement.

5. Lower the heels as far as is comfortable while keeping the torso erect and the knees straight.

Lower Body Workout | 121

Barbell Front Squat

ADVANCED

Instructions

1. Begin to lower the body into a deep squat with the weight descending down. Keep the spine long and the back tall and upright. You'll notice that the back stays almost completely vertical as you descend, unlike a traditional squat where the torso leans slightly forward.

EQUIPMENT

2. Your hips stay under the bar (rather than floating behind the bar in a traditional squat) even as your glutes continue to lower down below knee level. You'll also notice that the knees extend further out in front and the ankles flex more than in a traditional squat.

3. Keep the heels on the ground and your weight centered over the middle of your feet as you continue to descend. Try not to shift forward into the balls of the feet or back into the heels.

4. At the lowest position, your hamstrings will nearly touch the back of the calves. Keep elbows lifted at bar height (if possible) and chest upright to prevent the bar from rolling forward.

5. Reverse the squat in a slow, controlled manner with the hips and knees extending simultaneously. Continue lifting until the body is back at the starting position.

Tips and Notes!

Grip and elbow placement are key for proper form and safety.

Lower Body Workout | 123

Conclusion

A muscle is like a car—if you want it to run well, you have to warm it up! There are numerous health benefits associated with proper muscle building and strength training, especially for older adults. Due to the intimidating and confusing nature associated with strength training and the many different weights and tools used in exercises, many people over the age of 40 are reluctant to start strength training on their own. Acquiring a better understanding of getting into a sensible strength training program is important to developing a good strength training program.

Many people assume that working out is mainly about getting a more aesthetically pleasing physique. Therefore, while many in their twenties and thirties do have at least a basic working out routine in their everyday life, it tends to fade away as a person gets older. In reality, however, the need for consistent exercises increases with age, since metabolism has a direct correlation with physical activity, and it goes down during the aging process. Having too little muscle and too much fat on the body as an adult can lead to a plethora of health challenges after 40 such as cardiovascular disease, diabetes, osteoporosis, and even cancer. Strength training, in particular, has a great many advantages to an aging body. Aside from increasing metabolic rate, strength training helps replace muscles, reduce fat, decrease lower-back discomfort and arthritic pain varieties that are common among people after the age of 40, as well as boosting self-confidence.

Nutrition plays a great part in starting and maintaining a healthy strength training routine. Just like any other strength trainer or someone who engages in a muscle-building activity, adults over 40 also benefit from plenty of good proteins in their diet. A sound diet should go hand in hand with strength training exercises for them to work since a consistent workout program requires a large amount of both physical and mental energy. A good diet for strength training consists of generous amounts of lean meats, whole grains, fish, eggs, leafy greens, and more nutritious food. It is also equally important to avoid sugary snacks, deep-fried food, fizzy drinks, and other similar unhealthy food, which is anyway a necessary change in one's diet particularly after 40.

Getting into strength training is a gradual process. It should be treated more like a marathon, not a sprint. The introductory, beginner, and advanced level exercises mentioned in this book are to be considered as a guide that points you in the right direction, rather than a set program that is meant to be followed by everyone. Regardless of which stage you are in, there is no "perfect program" or a template that you can follow in order to get optimal results. It is all about trying out safe and proven exercises and finding out what works the best for you.

The type of exercise you do often does not matter as much as the level of effort and consistency that goes into it. The workouts mentioned in this book are solid and reliable and would give you a great start on your fitness journey. If you commit to them and persist with your training, you will eventually figure out the best program that works specifically for you. Good luck!

References

https://www.ncbi.nlm.nih.gov/pmc/articles/PMC4193807/

https://www.prevention.com/health/a20487687/10-ways-your-diet-should-change-after-40-according-to-nutritionists/

https://web.mit.edu/tkd/stretch/stretching_2.html

https://legionathletics.com/muscle-groups

 Because We Care About Our Readers.

Golden Lion Publications

Printed in Great Britain
by Amazon